Brokenly Beautiful

Marianne Nadal

Published by Marianne Nadal, 2024.

BROKENLY BEAUTIFUL

First edition. October 23, 2024.

ISBN: 979-8227852038

Written by Marianne Nadal.

Preface

My Story

I won't dive too deep into the details of my childhood—perhaps that's a story for another time—but I will focus on the moments that led me to Vince. Looking back, it feels like every step I took was leading me to him, and ultimately, to the person I am today.

As I reflect, I realize my courage and strength may have been shaped by the challenges I faced growing up. My family was far from perfect. My parents didn't always get along, and I witnessed things no child should—constant instability, deceit, troubles, chaos, etc. There were moments when we had all the comforts of life, only to lose it all and depend on family members just to get by. These experiences left me feeling unsteady, like I was always on shaky ground. But they also made me stronger. As a child, life often felt like a cycle of disappointment and uncertainty. Now, I see that those trials helped shape the resilience that defines me today. I don't believe you need to go through hardship to find strength, but I do believe in the incredible capacity humans have to overcome it. We have the power to rise from even the darkest places.

When I was 18, my family moved to United States. I never imagined my life would take me so far from home. I arrived with no plan, no grand vision of what my life should be. All I had was $50 in my pocket and no idea what the heck a bagel was. Transitioning from that bewildered young woman to someone managing responsibilities in this multi-billion tech industry with self-taught education and training was beyond my wildest dreams.

I met Vince unexpectedly when I turned 30, long before the days of swiping left or right on dating apps. At that point, I had nearly given up on the idea of "settling down" or getting married. I was never lucky when it came to love, so I stopped expecting it. Then, one evening, I found myself at a friend's 40th birthday party in Manhattan. As I waited for the rest of the crowd to arrive, there he was—this tall, slender man in a suit and red tie. My girlfriends thought he was really good looking, but at that moment, I wasn't in a place to notice. It wasn't that Vince wasn't attractive, but my mind was elsewhere.

Fate has a funny way of working. Vince and I didn't immediately become a couple. We were both in relationships at the time, but it didn't take long for our paths to cross again. And when we finally started dating, it wasn't some whirlwind romance—it was a slow, steady realization that we were meant to be. We moved in together, into his Elmwood Park bachelor pad, with no expectations and no plans. We were just together, and that was enough.

As we journeyed through life, we shared so many experiences—random travels, meaningful conversations, and even an unexpected proposal in Bermuda over a Long Island Iced Tea. There was no ring, no grand gesture—just us, in that moment. It was perfect. Vince never needed to do things by the book. And I loved that about him. Then we had our son Vinnie. We loved being parents, be bored and just doing the couple mundane things.

As life moved forward, we faced new challenges together, including the loss that still lingers in my heart today. Vince became sick, and in those final months, my world became a whirlwind of uncertainties, loss, confusion and hoping for a miracle. I held on to him as tightly as I could, trying to be strong for him, for us. But the hardest thing I've ever had to do was let him go.

Even now, the weight of those final moments is heavy. I can still feel the pain of holding his lifeless hand, trying to make sense of how everything had changed so quickly. But through the sorrow, I've learned that love doesn't end with loss. It evolves, shaping who you are and who you will become.

Our story—my story—didn't end with Vince's passing. It continues, as I navigate this life without him by my side. I carry his memory with me, woven into the very fabric of who I am. And though I am broken, I am still standing. I am "brokenly beautiful."

My Letter to Vince:

Dear Vince,

Though you are no longer here in body, your spirit and love continue to guide me. I feel your presence in the quiet moments, in the memories we shared, and in the lessons you left behind. In those echoes, I have found strength to carry on, and in the silence of your absence, I have discovered wisdom that I never knew I needed.

This book is a testament to you—to your life and to the love that endures far beyond the constraints of time. Even in your passing, you've shown me that beauty can rise from the deepest sorrow, and that love doesn't fade; it transforms.

Through you, I have learned that life is beautiful, even in its brokenness. You've taught me that even in loss, there is still light, and in pain, there is still grace. And in your son Vin, I see the beginnings of that same light. Though he is still young, I carry the hope that he will grow to reflect the kindness, strength, and love that you showed us all. I will do my best to help him become the man you would be proud of.

This journey of healing and this story I've written—both are forever intertwined with you, and through our son Vin, I hope your spirit will continue to shine brightly.

With love always,

Marianne

Dedication

To Melanie, Kat, Mike, Heather, Pete, Marty, Nina and the rest of my closest friends — your love and support have been unwavering, even when words failed. Thank you for walking this path with me.

To my mom Emer, stepdad Andre, my mother-in-law Jackie and my father in law Dr Vicente — your strength and unconditional love have guided me through the darkest times. I am forever grateful.

To my brothers Erik and Robby —you've been my pillars of strength, reminding me of the beauty in family bonds.

To my entire family specially Zarina, my sister-in-law Joann, my nephews and nieces Samantha, Gavin, Aiden, Adeline —you are my foundation, and I am so thankful for the love we share and for all your support.

To my only son Vinnie —your spirit, your laughter, your presence and your light give me hope every day. You are my greatest joy and my greatest reason to keep moving forward.

To Adam —your love and understanding have healed parts of me I didn't even know were broken. You've given me a safe space to grieve and to love again.

To Basia and Gage —thank you for welcoming me with open arms and for the warmth, your laughter and kindness you've shown me. Your presence is a gift.

To my neighbors in West Caldwell—your kindness, community, and support have made my journey a little easier. I am so grateful to be surrounded by such wonderful people.

To everyone special I met during the process of writing this ebook Martha, Melissa, Nikki, Madelyn — your stories, your encouragement, and your resilience have inspired me beyond words. You've reminded me that we are never truly alone in our grief.

Chapter 1: Introduction

Losing someone you love doesn't just change your world—it shatters it. The weight of grief, especially when sudden and unexpected, feels like an emotional earthquake, leaving cracks in the foundation of everything you once knew. It brings chaos, heartbreak, confusion, anger, and disbelief. No one is ever truly prepared for that kind of loss. I certainly wasn't. Three years ago, I lost Vince to a rare form of cancer, and in that moment, life as I knew it fell apart.

This book, "Brokenly Beautiful," is not written from the perspective of a psychologist or a professional healer. It's a raw, heartfelt account of my journey, penned by someone who has walked through the fire of grief and emerged—scarred, yes, but still standing. I share my story not to offer you answers, but to be a companion on your journey. This isn't a guide that tells you how to grieve; it's an invitation to feel every part of it, knowing you are not alone.

The sudden loss of Vince felt like a violent storm that tore through my life, leaving behind a broken, unfamiliar landscape. Our son Vinnie was only six, and suddenly, I was left to parent him alone, navigate the gaping void in our home, and confront a future that felt empty. In those early days, I was merely surviving—clinging to small routines, barely breathing—but slowly, step by step, I began to heal.

Two years after Vince's death, I experienced another blow: the early stages of breast cancer. It forced me to confront the fragility of life once more. This illness made me reflect on my strength and the resilience within me, even in the face of deep personal pain. These experiences reshaped my view of life, loss, and the power of healing.

This book is my way of reaching out to you, wherever you are in your grief. It's a testament to the human spirit's capacity to endure, to adapt, and to find light even in the darkest places. Yes, the journey through grief is painful, disorienting, and will test the limits of your strength. But it's also a journey that speaks to the depth of the love we shared with those we've lost. That love becomes the very thing that carries us forward.

Through these pages, I hope to remind you that there is no wrong way to grieve. You'll stumble, you'll rise, and you'll stumble again. But each time, you will rise a little stronger. Grief doesn't have to erase the beauty of your life. It may reshape it, redefine it, but through the cracks, you can find new beauty, a deeper appreciation for love, and eventually—peace.

"Brokenly Beautiful" is not just my story; it's a reflection of every heart that has felt the unbearable weight of loss and the incredible strength it takes to carry on. Together, let's walk this path—because no one should have to navigate this pain alone.

Chapter 2: A Personal Journey of Love and Loss

Loss is a force that shakes you to your core—a force that changes everything. When I experienced the depth of loss, it felt as though the ground beneath my feet had vanished. The future I had imagined, the life I had built or envisioned, suddenly became a memory—an unfinished story that no longer had a clear path. The days that followed were filled with a haze of grief and confusion, where even the smallest tasks felt insurmountable. How do you begin to rebuild when the very foundation of your life has crumbled?

Yet, as the fog of those days began to lift, I found that loss, as devastating as it was, did not mark the end. In fact, it revealed a new chapter—one that, though painful, was also deeply transformative. I came to understand that brokenness isn't the opposite of beauty; it is a part of it. The pieces of my shattered heart and life, once fragile and scattered, began to reveal a different kind of beauty—one that was born from the ashes of pain but pulsed with resilience, courage, and strength.

This book is about that journey—a journey of falling apart and finding my way back. It is about the power of hope, even when it seems impossible to grasp. It's about the beauty that lies within the cracks of our brokenness, showing us that we are not diminished by loss but reshaped by it.

Loss is not just the experience of death; it comes in many forms. It can be the end of a relationship that you once thought would last forever, the loss of a job or opportunity that defined a chapter of your life, or even the quiet loss of a version of yourself that you once knew and now must let go of. Grief doesn't follow a single path, and it rarely looks the way we expect it to. There were moments when I thought I would never feel joy again—times when I questioned whether I had the strength to carry on. But I came to realize that grief—whether from death, heartbreak, or personal failure—is not a sign of weakness. It is a testament to the depth of the connection we had to what was lost. The pain I carried was a reflection of the love, the dreams, the hopes I had held so deeply.

In mourning the things I had lost, I was also honoring the value they brought to my life. Over time, I learned that I could hold both: the sorrow of letting go and the gratitude for what those experiences gave me. In the darkest moments, I found an unexpected truth—loss and love are intertwined. They are two sides of the same coin, and through this, I discovered that what we lose doesn't simply disappear. It leaves an imprint on us, shaping who we are and how we move forward. Loss becomes part of our story, but it does not have to define its ending.

It was through this painful yet powerful realization that I found the strength to rebuild—not to recreate what was lost, but to embrace what still remained. I became stronger in ways I never imagined. My capacity for empathy deepened, my ability to connect with others grew richer, and my understanding of what it means to be human became more profound. The beauty of life doesn't disappear with loss—it evolves. It transforms into something deeper, something raw and real.

This journey is not about returning to the person I was before, but about embracing the person I have become. A person who has walked through fire and come out scarred, yes, but also forged by that fire into something stronger, more resilient, and more compassionate. I hope that as you read these words, you feel the courage within yourself to walk your own path of healing, knowing that even when the night feels endless, the dawn always comes.

You are not alone in your grief, whatever form it takes. And even in the midst of the greatest heartache, there is hope. You are not just surviving—you are learning to thrive in a new way. And in that thriving, there is a power, a beauty, and a strength that is uniquely yours to discover. You can rise again, not despite your loss, but because of it. You are more than your pain. You are more than your sorrow. You are a living testament to love's enduring legacy, and your journey, though marked by loss, is one of boundless hope and unshakable resilience.

Let this book serve as a reminder that loss, in all its forms, does not have the power to define you. It may change you, it may leave scars, but it also unlocks a strength and a beauty within you that was always there, waiting to be uncovered. You are more than what you have lost—you are what you choose to become because of it.

Chapter 3: The Layers of Grief

Grief isn't something you simply "get over." It's not a hurdle you leap over nor a phase you pass through and then return to life as it once was. Grief changes you. It becomes a part of your very being. It molds and reshapes you, and while it may not always be visible to the outside world, it lives within you—layered, complex, and ever-shifting. Some days it feels like a dull, constant ache, a subtle reminder of what you've lost. Other days, it crashes into you like a tidal wave, leaving you breathless and struggling to stay afloat.

But here's the truth: grief, though painful, is also powerful. It's a testament to the depth of what you held dear. It shows the magnitude of your love, your dreams, your hopes, and your losses. You grieve because you cared. You grieve because you loved. And that love doesn't just vanish—it transforms, becomes something deeper, something that stays with you even as you move forward.

Grief comes in layers. Some days, it feels like you're moving forward, finding your strength and rediscovering moments of peace. On other days, it feels like you've been dragged back into the deepest sorrow. This ebb and flow are part of the process. It's part of your journey. The beauty of grief is that it's not just about the sadness or the pain; it's also about the love, the memories, the joy that once was, and the life that still is.

In this chapter, I want to encourage you to embrace the layers of your grief. It's okay to feel it all—to feel the sadness, the anger, the confusion, and yes, even moments of joy in the same breath. Grief doesn't follow a straight line, and it doesn't have a timeline. It's messy. It's unpredictable. And that's okay. There is no "right" way to grieve, no perfect formula to follow. Your grief is as unique as your experiences and your losses, and that's what makes it meaningful.

Letting Grief Transform You

The idea of transformation might feel impossible when you're in the thick of your pain. I remember those early days, when every hour felt like a mountain I couldn't climb. But slowly, I began to realize that grief wasn't something I could conquer or outrun. It was something I had to allow myself to feel, to move through, and to let transform me.

Grief has the power to reshape us in profound ways. It can make us more compassionate, more understanding, and more deeply connected to the world around us. It can open our hearts to new experiences, new relationships, and new joys that we might not have been able to see before. Grief doesn't diminish who you are—it expands you, allowing you to see life with greater depth and clarity.

Each layer of grief has its own lesson to teach. Some days, the lesson is about patience—learning to give yourself time to heal. Other days, it's about resilience—finding the strength to keep going even when the weight feels unbearable. And sometimes, the lesson is simply about acceptance—allowing yourself to feel what you feel without judgment or expectation.

Grief is not something to be rushed through. Each layer deserves to be honored, acknowledged, and felt in its own time. Some layers will be easier to move through than others, and that's okay. The important thing is that you're allowing yourself to experience it fully, without trying to push it away or pretend it's not there.

Honoring Your Grief

Take a few moments each day to sit quietly and acknowledge the reality of your loss. You don't need to rush acceptance, but gently remind yourself that while this new reality is painful, you are strong enough to face it. Ask yourself: "What is this layer of grief teaching me today?" Write down whatever comes to mind, without judgment or expectation.

Over time, you may begin to see patterns, lessons, or moments of clarity that help you navigate your grief with more compassion and understanding.

As you move through the layers of your grief, remember that you are not alone. You are part of a larger journey, one that is shared by many who have also felt the weight of loss. Together, we are proof that while grief is painful, it also leads to growth, healing, and a deeper understanding of love.

Grief will change you, but it will not break you. And with time, you will find that within the layers of your grief, there is also hope. There is life. And there is always the possibility of joy waiting to be rediscovered. Keep going. You are stronger than you realize.

Chapter 4: Shock and Denial in Sudden Loss

When loss is sudden, the shock can be paralyzing. I remember the moment I was told Vince wouldn't make it. It was as if time stopped. The words felt distant and unreal, like they weren't meant for me. For weeks, I lived in a state of denial, unable to accept that he was really gone. I kept expecting to wake up from the nightmare, for life to return to the way it had been. But that didn't happen.

Denial is a natural part of grief. It's the mind's way of protecting us from the full weight of the loss. The shock acts like a buffer, giving us time to process the unthinkable in smaller, more manageable pieces. But eventually, the reality sinks in. And that's when the true work of healing begins.

In this chapter, we will explore the initial stages of grief—shock and denial—and how they manifest differently for each person. Sudden loss is one of the most disorienting experiences in life, and navigating those first weeks or months requires both patience and self-compassion. You may find yourself numb, struggling to believe what has happened, or even clinging to hope that it isn't real.

The Mind's Defense Mechanism

In those early days, denial can feel like a cocoon, keeping the overwhelming pain at bay. It's the mind's way of saying, "Not yet. You're not ready for this". There were days when I walked through life in a fog, going through the motions but feeling utterly disconnected from reality. I would hear people talk, see them laugh or cry, and it felt like I was watching them from a distance, as though I had been plucked from the world I once knew and dropped into some other version of life.

Denial isn't about refusing to accept the truth—it's about your brain giving you time to adjust. Sudden loss can feel like a violent rip in the fabric of your existence, and denial acts as a temporary patch, allowing you to navigate the days without collapsing under the weight of grief. And that's okay. If you're in denial, give yourself permission to stay there for a while. You don't have to rush into acceptance.

Moving Through the Shock

While denial may initially offer some protection, the reality of the loss eventually seeps in. You begin to realize that life, as you knew it, will never be the same. This realization can be terrifying and painful. The shock may ebb and flow; some days you might feel almost normal, while others may hit you like a tidal wave of sorrow.

It's important to allow yourself to move through the shock at your own pace. There's no timeline for how long it takes to transition from denial to acceptance. For some, it's a matter of weeks; for others, it may take months or longer. What's important is that you honor your process, without feeling pressured by others' expectations of when you should "move on."

Acknowledging the Reality of Loss

Take a few moments each day to sit quietly and acknowledge the reality of your loss. This doesn't mean forcing yourself to feel pain or sadness; it's about gently reminding yourself that this new reality, while painful, is something you can survive. You don't need to rush acceptance, but slowly, piece by piece, allow yourself to face what has happened.

For me, this looked like acknowledging small truths: "He's not going to walk through the door today," "We won't have dinner together tonight," or even "I'm here, and he's not." These were painful realizations, but they helped me start the process of accepting my new reality.

The Importance of Support

In the wake of sudden loss, it's easy to retreat inward, to isolate yourself from those around you. But this is when you need support the most. Whether it's friends, family, or a support group, having people to lean on during this time is crucial. They may not be able to take away the pain, but they can offer comfort, a listening ear, and a reminder that you're not alone.

Don't be afraid to reach out, even when you don't have the words to describe what you're feeling. Often, simply being in the presence of someone who cares can help ease the burden, even if only for a moment.

Shock and denial are natural, necessary parts of the grieving process. They're not signs of weakness, nor are they something to be rushed through. Take your time. Allow yourself the space to come to terms with your new reality. And remember, no matter how distant or disconnected you feel, you are not alone. You are still here. You are still breathing. And in time, the shock will subside, and you'll find the strength to continue forward.

Chapter 5: Giving Yourself Permission to Grieve

Grief is not a one-size-fits-all experience. It's a profoundly personal journey that we each must walk in our own way, at our own pace. In a world that often tries to rush us through discomfort or offer quick fixes, the importance of creating space to fully grieve cannot be overstated. This chapter is about honoring your unique path through grief and giving yourself permission to feel, to heal, and to experience this process on your own terms.

Your Grief, Your Path

No one else can dictate how you should grieve, nor can they truly understand the depth of your experience. Grief, in whatever form it takes—loss of a loved one, a relationship, a job, a dream—is deeply individual. It might not fit any preconceived notions or follow the timeline others expect, and that's perfectly okay. Your grief is as unique as your relationship to what you've lost. It's essential to honor that.

I remember feeling inundated by advice from well-meaning friends and family after my loss. They told me how I "should" grieve, how I should handle the pain, and what I needed to do to "feel better." Their intentions were kind, but I often felt like I was failing. It was as though I wasn't grieving the "right" way. The moment I realized that there "is" no right way, I began to take back my power. My grief was my own, and it was okay to experience it on my terms.

Letting Go of the "Shoulds"

Along this journey, you might be bombarded with ideas of how you "should" feel, what you "should" do, and how quickly you "should" move on. But here's a powerful truth: there is no "should" when it comes to grieving. There is no rulebook for this experience, no clear path you must follow. Grief isn't a problem to be solved or a task to be completed—it's an emotional process that deserves space. It's more than okay to carve out your own path and to walk that path at your own pace. There is no finish line, no deadline to meet, and no expectation you have to live up to.

Grieving on Your Own Timeline

Time moves differently when you're grieving. Some days may feel endless, while others might pass in a blur. Some people may find that the sharpness of their pain softens more quickly, while others feel its intensity for months, even years. Both experiences are valid. There is no stopwatch on grief. I had days where I felt a sense of peace, thinking I was finally moving forward, only to be blindsided by a wave of sadness the next. It's a rollercoaster—full of highs and lows—and I had to remind myself that this was all part of the process. Healing does not happen in a straight line.

Welcoming All Your Emotions

Grief is messy. It brings with it a whirlwind of emotions—sadness, anger, confusion, guilt, and sometimes even relief or moments of joy. It's okay to feel everything, even if it doesn't make sense. It's okay to cry, to scream, to laugh, to feel numb. Let yourself experience these emotions fully without judgment. This is your healing process, and every emotion you feel is part of that. Denying yourself the opportunity to feel only delays your healing. Grief isn't just about sadness—it's about the entire spectrum of human emotions that come with loss.

In my own journey through grief, I often felt guilty for feeling moments of joy. When I laughed or felt a spark of happiness, it was immediately followed by a wave of guilt—how could I be happy when I was grieving? But I learned that grief and joy can coexist. One does not cancel out the other. Grief may be ever-present, but that doesn't mean there isn't room for joy. Over time, I allowed myself to embrace both.

Embracing Your Emotions

Take a few moments to write down all the emotions you're feeling, without filtering them. Maybe you're angry, sad, relieved, or confused. Maybe you feel all of these things at once. Allow yourself to feel everything, knowing that every emotion is valid and that this is all part of your unique healing journey.

Grief is not a journey with a clear destination. It's a process that unfolds in its own time and in its own way. As you move through it, give yourself permission to feel everything—whether it's sadness, anger, or even moments of joy. This is your path, and you are allowed to walk it in whatever way feels right for you. You are not broken beyond repair. You are "brokenly beautiful", and each day, you are finding new ways to heal.

Chapter 6: Self-Care During Grief

Grief has a way of consuming everything. It seeps into your thoughts, your body, your spirit, leaving you feeling emotionally and physically exhausted. In moments of intense loss, it can feel impossible to focus on anything else. The world around you fades, and the simple act of getting through the day becomes an enormous challenge. That's why self-care is not just important—it's essential. During the hardest days of grief, self-care becomes a lifeline, a way to remind yourself that you are still worthy of care, love, and kindness, even in your brokenness.

When we think of self-care, it's easy to imagine elaborate routines, spa days, or indulgent practices. But in the midst of grief, self-care often looks very different. It's about meeting your most basic needs—ensuring you eat, sleep, and find small moments of peace amidst the chaos. It's about carving out time for yourself, no matter how small, to breathe, to rest, and to find solace in the act of taking care of your heart, your body, and your mind.

Relearning to Take Care of Yourself

When you're deep in grief, the idea of caring for yourself can feel overwhelming. You might wonder, "What's the point?" or "How can I focus on myself when I feel this broken?" But here's the truth: taking care of yourself isn't selfish. It's survival. It's allowing yourself the space to heal, one moment at a time.

After my own loss, I found that self-care didn't come easily. I was so focused on my pain that I forgot to tend to my own needs. I wasn't eating regularly. Sleep was a distant memory. And I certainly wasn't allowing myself any moments of peace or joy. But as time passed, I realized that in order to survive, I had to start taking care of myself again—slowly, gently, and with great compassion.

The Basics: Sleep, Nutrition, and Movement

When everything feels like it's falling apart, focusing on the basics can help ground you. Ensuring that you get enough sleep, nourishing your body with food, and moving in ways that feel gentle and healing are foundational acts of self-care. In the midst of grief, these may feel like monumental tasks, but they are essential.

Grief can wreak havoc on your sleep patterns. Insomnia or disrupted sleep is common when your heart and mind are in turmoil. Creating a calming bedtime routine can help. Whether it's reading, meditating, or simply taking a few deep breaths, these small rituals can prepare your body for rest. Don't be afraid to reach out to a professional if you're struggling to sleep—your body needs rest to heal.

Grief often takes away your appetite. You might feel like eating is the last thing on your mind, but nourishing your body with food is crucial. Start small—keep it simple. Even something as basic as a smoothie or a handful of fruit can make a difference. Eating is a way of reminding your body that it still matters, that you are still here, even when everything feels overwhelming.

Grief can make you feel heavy, like the weight of the world is pressing down on you. But movement, even gentle movement, can help lift some of that weight. It's not about pushing your body to its limits—it's about reconnecting with it. A walk, some light stretching, or even a slow yoga practice can be surprisingly healing. I found that taking short walks in nature, even when I didn't feel like it, gave me moments of peace.

Carving Out Moments for You

Self-care doesn't have to be complicated. It's about finding small moments in the day to nurture yourself. Maybe it's soaking in a warm bath, sitting in quiet meditation, or simply taking a few deep breaths when everything feels overwhelming. These moments are gifts you give yourself—gifts that remind you that you are still worthy of care, even in your most broken moments.

Take a few moments to create a simple self-care plan for your day. It doesn't have to be big. Maybe it's as small as drinking water, taking a few deep breaths, or getting outside for a few minutes of fresh air. Be kind to yourself—these small acts of care add up over time.

Self-care during grief is not about escaping the pain. It's about honoring yourself as you navigate it. Grief, in all its forms, is exhausting. But you are still here, still worthy of care, still deserving of love and compassion. As you continue to journey through this book, remember that taking care of yourself is one of the most powerful ways to move through your grief. You are brokenly beautiful, and through each act of self-care, you are choosing to heal.

Chapter 7: Finding Support

Grief can feel like a long, solitary road, no matter what kind of loss you're experiencing— a sudden shift in your life's direction, or the passing of someone you love. It's a journey filled with twists and turns, ups and downs, and moments where the darkness seems endless. But here's the truth: you don't have to walk this road alone. Finding support is like discovering a lantern in the night—it doesn't take away the darkness, but it illuminates a path forward.

In this chapter, we'll explore how different forms of support—from close friends and family to therapy and support groups—can become your guiding lights.

Your Circle of Empathy

Imagine walking into a room where everyone speaks the language of loss—where the people around you "get it" in a way that others might not. That's what support groups offer—a circle of empathy where your feelings are not just acknowledged but shared. There's something powerful about being in a space where your experiences are mirrored in others.

Support groups offer more than just sympathy—they offer understanding. You're invited to let your guard down, to speak your heart without fear of judgment. In these spaces, you'll find practical advice, shared stories, and the reassurance that what you're feeling is valid. Whether it's an in-person meetup or an online community focused on your specific kind of loss, there's a space waiting for you—a space where you can begin to heal in the presence of others who understand your journey.

For me, joining a support group for bereaved spouses was a turning point. I wasn't just grieving the loss of Vince; I was grieving the future we had planned, the life we were supposed to live. In that group, I found people who had walked a similar path, and hearing their stories made me feel less alone. We cried together, laughed together, and found strength in our shared experiences. Knowing that others had survived gave me hope that I could too.

Your Compassionate Guide

Grief is complicated, no matter what form it takes. And sometimes even the most supportive friends and family can't help you untangle the emotional knots that grief ties inside you. That's where therapy comes in—a compassionate guide to help you navigate the fog.

Therapists offer a safe space to express your emotions without judgment, helping you process the layers of your grief and move forward. In therapy, you can begin to understand your grief, not as something to "fix," but as something to live with and grow through.

One of the hardest parts of grief is admitting that you need help. There's a natural instinct to withdraw, to isolate, to "handle it" on your own. But true courage lies in asking for help when you need it.

Reaching out for support doesn't make you weak—it shows your strength. It takes courage to say, "I'm not okay," and to let others in on your journey. When you allow others to help you, you're not only giving yourself the gift of support, but you're also giving them the opportunity to show their love and care for you. Vulnerability creates space for others to show up for you, just as you've shown up for them in the past.

Allowing Yourself to Be Held

There's profound healing in allowing yourself to be held—physically, emotionally, and spiritually. Letting yourself be held might look like accepting a friend's offer to cook you dinner, or letting your family take care of practical things, like running errands. It might mean joining a support group or seeking out a therapist who can guide you through the rough terrain of your grief.

Allowing yourself to be supported is not a sign of weakness—it's a testament to your resilience. Grief is too heavy to carry alone, and by opening yourself up to support, you're giving yourself permission to heal.

As you continue this journey, remember that you don't have to carry the weight of your grief alone. There are people—whether friends, family, or professionals—ready to walk with you, to lift you up, and to remind you that even in the midst of your loss, you are never truly alone. You are "brokenly beautiful", and by leaning on your support system, you're taking the first steps toward healing.

Chapter 8: The Power of Vulnerability

Vulnerability is often misunderstood as a weakness, especially in the face of grief. We are told to "be strong," to keep it together for the sake of others, and to hide the depth of our pain behind a brave face. But in reality, vulnerability is one of the greatest strengths you can possess, particularly when dealing with loss.

Grief cracks us open in ways we never anticipated, leaving us raw, exposed, and deeply vulnerable. I remember trying to hold everything together, to be strong for everyone else, to keep my tears hidden and my emotions under control. But the true strength didn't come from hiding my pain. The real strength emerged when I allowed myself to fall apart, to be vulnerable, and to let others witness my brokenness. That's when the healing truly began.

This chapter is about embracing vulnerability—letting go of the idea that you need to "have it all together." It's about recognizing that showing your pain, asking for help, and being honest with yourself and others is not weakness—it's an act of courage. Vulnerability allows you to connect with others in the most authentic way, and through that connection, you find the strength to heal.

The Courage of Being Seen

We often think that strength means holding everything inside, not letting others see the cracks in our armor. But real strength lies in allowing yourself to be seen exactly as you are—broken pieces and all. It's in those moments, when you admit you're hurting, when you share your truth, when you let others see your pain, that the deepest connections are formed. And those connections are where healing begins.

Vulnerability is not a burden on those who love you. It's an invitation for them to stand beside you, to help carry the weight of your grief, and to remind you that you don't have to carry it all by yourself. When I let my guard down, I realized that the people around me didn't see me as weak—they saw me as human. That human connection is one of the most powerful tools for healing.

Asking for Help

One of the hardest parts of grief is admitting that you need help. There's often a natural instinct to withdraw, to isolate, to "handle it" on your own. But true courage lies in asking for help when you need it.

Reaching out for support doesn't make you weak—it shows your strength. It takes courage to say, "I'm not okay," and to let others be part of your journey. When you allow others to help you, you're not only giving yourself the gift of support, but you're also giving them the opportunity to show their love and care for you. Vulnerability creates the space for others to show up for you, just as you've shown up for them in the past.

Allowing Yourself to Be Held

There's a profound sense of healing in allowing yourself to be held—physically, emotionally, and spiritually. Letting yourself be held might mean accepting a friend's offer to bring you a meal, or letting your family help with practical things like running errands. It could mean leaning on a support group or working with a therapist who can guide you through the roughest terrain of your grief.

Allowing yourself to be supported is not a sign of weakness—it's a testament to your resilience. Grief is too heavy to carry alone, and by opening yourself up to support, you're giving yourself permission to heal.

Practicing Vulnerability

The next time you're tempted to say, "I'm fine" when you're struggling, pause. Consider telling the truth about how you're feeling, even if it feels uncomfortable. Practice asking for help, even in small ways, and notice how others respond. You may be surprised by the strength and connection that vulnerability brings into your life.

Vulnerability is not the end of your strength—it's the beginning. When you allow yourself to be vulnerable, to show your brokenness, you are opening yourself up to healing. It's in those raw, vulnerable moments that you will find your true strength—the strength to move forward, to heal, and to connect deeply with the world around you. You are "brokenly beautiful", and in your vulnerability lies your power.

Chapter 9: Self-Care for the Grieving Soul

Grief has a way of consuming you completely. It seeps into every part of your being, making the simplest tasks feel monumental. When you're deep in it, the idea of self-care can seem distant, even frivolous. How can you take care of yourself when the weight of your sorrow feels like it's crushing you? But here's the truth: self-care is not a luxury in times of grief—it's a lifeline. It's one of the most loving things you can do for yourself, even when it feels like you have nothing left to give.

In my own journey through loss, I discovered that self-care wasn't about grand gestures or routines. It was about small, simple acts of kindness toward myself—things that helped me feel grounded, that reminded me I was still here, still deserving of care, even in my brokenness. Grief may demand your attention, but you are allowed to carve out space for yourself within it. In fact, you must.

Nurturing Your Body Through Pain

Grief doesn't just affect your heart and mind—it takes a toll on your body, too. The weight of sorrow can leave you feeling exhausted, and sleep may seem like a distant memory. Your appetite may vanish, or you might find yourself turning to food for comfort. Grief has a way of disrupting every part of you. That's why taking care of your physical self is so essential, even when it feels impossible.

Maybe that means starting with the basics—ensuring you're drinking enough water, eating a little bit of nourishing food, or stepping outside for a few minutes to feel the sunlight on your skin. These small acts of care, though they may seem insignificant in the face of your pain, are powerful. They remind you that you are still here, still worthy of love, even when you feel broken beyond repair.

Rest as an Act of Love

When grief keeps you awake at night, when your mind races and your heart aches, rest may seem out of reach. But rest is not a luxury—it's an act of love toward yourself. Creating a simple bedtime routine can become a sacred ritual, a way to care for yourself in the quiet moments when the world feels the most heavy.

- Set a Routine: Even if everything else in your life feels chaotic, having a consistent bedtime and wake-up time can bring some comfort. Your body craves rhythm, especially when your heart is in turmoil.

- Create a Peaceful Space: Turn your bedroom into a sanctuary. Soft lighting, clean sheets, a comforting scent—these small touches can create a space that feels safe, even when your emotions feel overwhelming.

- Unplug and Unwind: Before bed, try to unplug from the world. Set aside your phone, step away from the screens, and give yourself time to breathe. These moments of quiet are not about escaping your grief—they're about giving yourself the strength to face it again tomorrow.

Rest doesn't mean forgetting your pain. It's about honoring your need for care, even when everything inside you feels raw and exposed.

Movement as Medicine

Grief can make you feel like the weight of the world is pressing down on you. But movement, even the gentlest kind, can help lighten that burden. It's not about pushing yourself or forcing your body to do more than it can handle. It's about reconnecting with yourself, even in the smallest of ways.

In the early days of my grief, I started taking short walks. At first, it felt pointless, as if nothing could pull me out of the fog. But slowly, with each step, I began to feel more present in the world around me. The fresh air, the movement, the act of putting one foot in front of the other—it didn't erase my pain, but it reminded me that life still existed, even in the midst of my sorrow.

Creating Space for Small Moments of Care

Self-care doesn't have to be complicated or time-consuming. It's about finding small, quiet moments in your day where you can nurture yourself. Maybe it's sitting in a warm bath, wrapping yourself in a blanket, or simply taking a deep breath when everything feels overwhelming. These small acts are not about escaping your grief—they're about reminding yourself that you are still deserving of care, even when it feels like the world has forgotten you.

A Gentle Self-Care Plan

Take a moment to create a simple self-care plan for yourself. It doesn't have to be elaborate or perfect. It might be as small as drinking water, breathing deeply, or stepping outside for a few moments of fresh air. Be kind to yourself—these small acts of care are building blocks for your healing.

Self-care during grief is not about escaping the pain. It's about honoring your needs as you move through it. Grief, in all its forms, is exhausting. But you are still here. You are still worthy of love, of rest, of care. You are *brokenly beautiful*, and through each small act of self-care, you are choosing to heal, one breath at a time.

Chapter 10: Leaning on Your Support System

Grief has a way of isolating you. It feels like you're walking through a dense fog, lost and alone. The weight of that pain can feel unbearable. I know this feeling too well. I thought I had to be strong, to bear the brunt of my grief in silence. But here's the truth I wish I had learned sooner: strength doesn't come from suffering alone—it comes from knowing when to lean on others.

No one should have to navigate loss by themselves. The journey through grief—whether it's the loss of a person, a future, or a part of your identity—is not one you're meant to walk alone. I learned this the hard way. For a long time, I kept my pain to myself, believing that if I just held on a little longer, if I could push through, I would somehow come out the other side. But all that did was leave me exhausted and even more disconnected from the people who could have helped me carry the burden.

It wasn't until I allowed others in—truly let them in—that I began to heal. There is incredible power in vulnerability, and there is undeniable strength in allowing yourself to be supported by the people who care about you. This chapter is about that process—about building your support system, learning to communicate your needs, and letting yourself be held in the most fragile moments.

You Are Not a Burden

One of the hardest lessons I had to learn was this: "You are not a burden". When you're deep in grief—it's easy to convince yourself that your pain is too much for others to bear. You might worry that sharing your grief will only add to their load, that you'll be seen as a burden. But let me remind you: the people who love you "want" to be there for you. They want to support you. And letting them in isn't weakness—it's an act of strength.

Grief convinces us that we have to bear the weight alone, that showing our pain makes us weak. But nothing could be further from the truth. Letting others see your vulnerability, allowing them to hold you when you can't hold yourself—that's one of the bravest things you can do. It's not about dumping your pain onto someone else; it's about sharing the load, about letting the people who care about you stand beside you in your darkest moments.

Building Your Support System

A support system is like a safety net that catches you when the weight of grief becomes too heavy to carry alone. This net can take many forms—it might be family, friends, colleagues, a support group, or even a therapist. What matters most is that you have people you can turn to, people who understand that grief doesn't follow a straight line—that it's messy, complicated, and deeply personal.

Start by identifying the people in your life who make you feel safe. Who can you be yourself with, without fear of judgment? Who listens—truly listens—when you talk about your pain? These are the people who can form the foundation of your support system. Sometimes, your network will expand beyond your immediate circle. Support groups, whether in person or online, offer a space to connect with others who are walking a similar path. In these spaces, you don't have to explain yourself; you don't have to justify your feelings. You can simply *be*, and that can be a profound source of comfort.

Communicating Your Needs

Learning to ask for help can be one of the most challenging aspects of grief. We often assume that others should know what we need, that if they truly cared, they'd understand our pain without us having to say a word. But the reality is, even the people who love us most can't read our minds. They want to help, but they might not know how.

Take some time to reflect on what you need. Do you need someone to simply listen? Do you need practical help, like someone to take care of errands or tasks? Do you need space, or do you need company? Whatever it is, try to communicate your needs as clearly as you can. It might feel uncomfortable at first, but remember: the people who care about you want to support you—they just need to know how.

Allowing Yourself to Be Held

There's a profound healing that comes from allowing yourself to be held—physically, emotionally, and spiritually. Letting yourself be held might mean accepting a friend's offer to cook you dinner or allowing your family to take care of the practical things. It could mean joining a support group or finding a therapist who can guide you through the pain.

Allowing yourself to be supported isn't weakness—it's an act of resilience. Grief is too heavy to carry alone, and by opening yourself up to support, you're giving yourself permission to heal.

Reaching Out Isn't Always Easy, But It's Worth It

Reaching out for support takes courage. It requires vulnerability, and that can feel risky when you're already hurting. But healing doesn't happen in isolation—it happens in connection. When you reach out—whether to a friend, a family member, or a support group—you're taking a step toward healing, toward finding light in the midst of your pain.

You are not a burden. The people who love you want to support you, and letting them in is an act of strength, not weakness. It's okay to lean on others. It's okay to ask for help. You don't have to carry this alone.

Healing begins when we allow ourselves to be held—by those who care, by our support systems, and by the belief that we are worthy of love, even in our brokenness.

In this journey of grief, whatever form your loss has taken, remember that you are not alone. There are people ready to support you, to help carry the weight, to walk beside you. You are "brokenly beautiful", and by leaning on your support system, you're taking the first steps toward healing, toward finding light in the midst of your darkest days. Let yourself be held—you deserve that now more than ever.

Chapter 11: Finding Purpose Through Pain

Grief has a way of completely shattering the life you once knew. The pain can feel unbearable, leaving you asking, "What now? What do I do with all of this?" I remember standing in the aftermath of Vince's passing, feeling like the ground had been ripped from beneath me. Life as I had known it was gone. And in the silence that followed, a question echoed in my heart: "Where do I go from here?"

Grief changes you. It forces you to confront parts of yourself you didn't even know existed. It makes you reevaluate everything—your values, your relationships, your sense of purpose. There's a rawness in grief that strips away all the noise, leaving you face-to-face with your truest self. In those early days, I couldn't see beyond the pain. I couldn't imagine a future where I'd feel anything but heartache. But slowly, painfully, I began to realize that grief, while devastating, can also be a catalyst for transformation. It opened my heart to new possibilities, new ways of seeing the world, and ultimately new ways of finding purpose.

This chapter is about that journey—the journey of finding purpose through pain. It's about how the very things that break us can also lead us to a deeper understanding of ourselves, of the world, and of what truly matters. It's not about turning pain into something pretty or pretending that everything happens for a reason. It's about honoring your grief, holding space for it, and allowing it to shape you into someone stronger, wiser, and more compassionate than you ever thought possible.

Grief as a Catalyst for Change

When you're in the depths of grief, it's hard to see beyond the pain. It's hard to imagine that anything good could come from something so devastating. But here's the thing: grief forces you to change. It strips away the layers of your life that no longer serve you. It shakes up everything you thought you knew about yourself and the world. And in that upheaval, there's an opportunity for transformation.

After Vince died, I found myself questioning everything—my purpose, my goals, even my sense of self. I had to rebuild not just my life, but my entire identity. And while that process was painful, it was also incredibly powerful. Grief gave me permission to let go of things that no longer fit and to create space for something new.

Finding Purpose in the Pain

One of the hardest parts of grief is the feeling of being untethered, as if the foundation of your life has crumbled beneath you. The future you once envisioned feels out of reach, and you're left wondering, "What's next?" But here's what I learned: purpose doesn't disappear in the wake of loss—it shifts.

You might not be able to return to the life you once knew, but you can find new meaning in the life that's unfolding before you. For me, that meant embracing my grief, allowing it to teach me new lessons about myself and the world. I found purpose in writing, in connecting with others who were also grieving, and in sharing my story so that others wouldn't feel alone.

You may find purpose in different ways—in helping others, in honoring the memory of what you've lost, or in rediscovering passions that had been buried under the weight of grief. The key is to remain open to the possibility that purpose can exist alongside your pain.

Honoring What Was Lost While Embracing What Is

Finding purpose through grief doesn't mean forgetting what you've lost. It doesn't mean moving on or leaving the past behind. Instead, it means finding a way to honor what was while making room for what is. You can carry your grief with you while also creating a life that feels meaningful.

For me, honoring Vince's memory became a cornerstone of my healing. I didn't have to forget him in order to move forward. Instead, I found ways to incorporate his memory into my new life. You don't have to let go of what was in order to embrace what is.

A New Chapter, A New Purpose

The beauty of grief is that it opens the door to a new chapter. It allows you to redefine your purpose in ways you may never have considered before. It may be scary, and it may feel uncertain, but in the midst of that uncertainty, there is potential for something beautiful.

As you move forward in your grief, give yourself permission to explore new possibilities. You don't have to have it all figured out right now. The path will unfold as you take each step. And with each step, you are creating a life that honors both what you've lost and what you still have.

Grief is not the end of your story. It is the beginning of a new chapter—one that is filled with both pain and purpose. You are not just surviving; you are transforming. You are becoming someone stronger, someone wiser, and someone who can carry both the weight of your loss and the beauty of your life. You are "brokenly beautiful", and in that brokenness, you will find the strength to create a life that is full of meaning and purpose.

Chapter 12: The Importance of Therapy

Therapy was a game-changer for me, but it wasn't always easy to admit I needed it. For the longest time, I resisted the idea of asking for help. I thought I could manage my grief on my own—that I was strong enough to handle the pain without leaning on anyone else. But that mindset kept me trapped in a cycle of isolation and despair, and it wasn't until I opened the door to professional help that I began to truly heal.

Grief can take many forms. It's not always about losing a loved one. It can be the end of a relationship, the loss of a career, or the crumbling of a future you once envisioned. Whatever shape it takes, grief has a way of overwhelming you, making you feel as though you're drowning in a sea of emotions with no way out. That's where therapy comes in—not as a way to "fix" your grief, but as a space where you can unpack it, process it, and learn to live with it in a healthy, constructive way.

Why We Resist Therapy

So many of us resist therapy because we think asking for help is a sign of weakness. I grew up believing that strength meant being able to handle everything on my own, without showing vulnerability. When I lost Vince, I thought if I could just survive each day without breaking down, that was enough. But I was wrong.

The truth is, trying to carry the weight of grief by yourself doesn't make you stronger. It just makes the load heavier. There is no shame in seeking help. In fact, it takes incredible courage to say, "I can't do this alone". Therapy became a turning point for me—a place where I didn't have to pretend to be okay, where I could let my guard down and truly begin to heal.

What Therapy Offers

Therapy provides something that friends and family, no matter how well-intentioned, often can't: a neutral, supportive space where you can explore your feelings without fear of judgment. It offers tools to help you understand your grief, navigate the emotions it brings, and ultimately begin to heal. My therapist helped me untangle the web of emotions I was feeling—anger, sadness, guilt, confusion—and guided me in learning how to cope with them in a healthy way.

One of the most valuable things therapy gave me was the realization that it's okay to feel everything—there is no "right" way to grieve. Therapy gives you the tools to process that loss on your own terms. It helps you recognize that the waves of grief, while painful, are part of the healing process.

The Strength in Vulnerability

When you're grieving, it's easy to put up walls. You don't want others to see how much you're hurting. But in therapy, those walls come down. You're allowed to be vulnerable, to cry, to express your anger and your sorrow without holding anything back. And that vulnerability? It's not a weakness—it's a strength.

Being vulnerable in therapy was one of the hardest, but most important, things I ever did. It allowed me to let go of the pressure to "have it all together" and embrace the messiness of my emotions. In doing so, I found a new kind of strength—a strength that didn't come from pretending I was okay, but from acknowledging that I wasn't.

Therapy as a Lifeline

For me, therapy was more than just a place to talk—it became a lifeline. It was where I found guidance when I felt lost, hope when I thought I had none left, and the strength to keep moving forward, even on the darkest days. It wasn't a quick fix, but it gave me the tools I needed to rebuild my life after loss.

Grief is not something you can fix or get over—it's something you learn to live with. And therapy helps you do just that. It provides you with the skills to navigate your grief, to find meaning in your pain, and to create a future that honors both what you've lost and what still lies ahead.

If you're struggling with grief, I encourage you to consider therapy. It's not a sign of weakness to ask for help—it's a declaration of your commitment to yourself. Therapy is a space where you can begin to heal, to process your emotions, and to move forward with a renewed sense of strength and purpose.

In this journey of grief, therapy can offer a beacon of light in the darkness. It's a place where you can explore your feelings, find support, and begin the work of healing. You are "brokenly beautiful", and through therapy, you can find the courage to honor your grief while also finding hope for the future. Healing isn't about erasing the pain—it's about learning how to live with it, and therapy can help you do just that.

Chapter 13: Navigating Social Events and Celebrations

Grief changes everything, especially how you experience the world around you. After any significant loss—social events can feel almost unbearable. It's like the world is moving forward, celebrating, laughing, and continuing as usual, while you're left grappling with the weight of your pain, unsure how to rejoin the flow of life.

I remember my first holiday season after Vince passed. The thought of Christmas without him felt impossible. How could I celebrate? How could I smile when his absence was the only thing I could feel? Every tradition, every song, every decoration felt like a painful reminder of what was missing. I wanted to hide away from it all, to retreat from the world that seemed to be carrying on, blissfully unaware of the void in my heart. But I learned, slowly and painfully, that there are ways to navigate these moments without abandoning your grief. It's not about forcing yourself to be joyful or pretending that everything is okay. It's about finding a balance between honoring your loss and allowing yourself to step into the present, even if it feels fragile.

This chapter is for anyone who has struggled with social events or celebrations after a loss of any kind. There are ways to approach these moments that honor both your grief and the possibility of joy.

The Complexity of Mixed Emotions

One of the hardest things to accept after loss is that joy and grief can coexist. I used to think that if I allowed myself to enjoy something—whether it was a family gathering, a birthday party, or even just a quiet moment of laughter—it somehow meant I was betraying my grief. It felt like acknowledging happiness would minimize the depth of what I had lost. But here's the truth: you can feel both. You "are" allowed to feel both.

Grief doesn't cancel out joy, and joy doesn't erase grief. They live side by side, sometimes in the same moment. I remember sitting at a holiday dinner, surrounded by family, feeling the weight of Vince's absence like a shadow over everything. But then, in a moment of unexpected laughter with the kids, I realized something: it was okay to laugh. It was okay to find a spark of light, even in the midst of the darkness. My grief was still there, as present as ever, but so was the love, the connection, and the possibility of healing.

When you're mourning, you don't have to choose between your sadness and your joy. Both can exist within you, and both are valid.

Setting Boundaries and Creating New Traditions

One of the most important lessons I learned was that I didn't have to do things the way I had always done them. If the idea of attending a large holiday gathering feels overwhelming, it's okay to say no. If certain traditions feel too painful, you have the power to change them. Navigating social events after a loss means giving yourself permission to do things differently. It's about recognizing what you need in each moment and creating boundaries that protect your emotional well-being.

For me, that first Christmas without Vince was excruciating. The thought of putting up the same decorations, sitting around the same table, and trying to celebrate the same way felt impossible. So, I didn't. Instead of forcing myself into old traditions, I created new ones—ones that honored his memory while also allowing me to breathe. We lit candles in his honor, shared stories, but we also allowed ourselves to laugh, to embrace the moments of connection that still existed.

It's important to remember that your grief is yours, and you get to decide how you move through it. If that means stepping back from certain events, do it. If it means creating new traditions or reimagining old ones, do it. There is no right or wrong way to navigate these moments. The only thing that matters is what feels right for you.

Planning Ahead and Asking for Support

One of the best things you can do for yourself is to plan ahead. Anticipating difficult events or social gatherings can help reduce some of the anxiety that comes with the unknown. Ask yourself: What do I need to feel comfortable? What boundaries do I need to set? Who can I lean on for support?

For me, that meant talking to my family before the holidays and letting them know where I was emotionally. I needed them to understand that I might not be fully present, that I might need to step away, and that it was okay if I wasn't my usual self. Communicating these needs ahead of time allowed me to feel less pressure and more supported.

It's also okay to ask for help. If you're struggling, reach out to someone you trust. Let them know what you're feeling. Maybe it's a friend who can be your anchor at a social event, or maybe it's a family member who can help you create space for quiet moments when things feel overwhelming. You don't have to navigate these occasions alone.

Giving Yourself Permission to Step Back

Just because you're invited to an event doesn't mean you have to go. And just because you attend a celebration doesn't mean you have to stay the whole time. Give yourself permission to step back when you need to. Sometimes, the best way to honor your grief is to allow yourself space to retreat, to say no, or to leave early without guilt.

After my loss, I realized that I didn't have to force myself into situations that felt too overwhelming. If a social gathering was too much, I allowed myself to skip it. If I attended an event and felt the need to leave, I did. And each time, I reminded myself that it was okay. There is strength in knowing your limits and in protecting your heart when it feels too fragile.

Honoring Both the Grief and the Joy

At the heart of navigating social events and celebrations after loss is the idea that both grief and joy can be honored. It's okay to bring your grief with you to the table. It's okay to speak about it, to acknowledge it, and to let it be part of the conversation. And it's okay to embrace moments of happiness, too.

One year, during a family gathering, we decided to make a toast to the people we had lost. It was a simple moment, but it brought both the grief and the love to the surface. We cried, we laughed, and in that shared experience, I felt a sense of healing. We weren't pretending that everything was okay, but we were allowing the complexity of life—of loss and love, of sadness and joy—to exist together.

Plan ahead for upcoming holidays or social events. Think about what you need to feel comfortable, and don't be afraid to set boundaries or ask for support. Consider how you might honor your grief while also allowing yourself to engage with the present moment. Maybe that means creating a new tradition, or maybe it means giving yourself permission to skip certain events altogether. Whatever you decide, trust that it's the right decision for you.

Social events and celebrations after loss are never easy, but they don't have to be impossible. By finding balance, setting boundaries, and allowing both your grief and your joy to coexist, you can navigate these moments in a way that honors where you are in your healing journey. Remember, you are *brokenly beautiful*, and in the complexity of your emotions, there is both strength and grace. It's okay to step back when you need to, and it's okay to step forward when you're ready. Both are acts of courage.

Chapter 14: The Journey of Acceptance

Acceptance. It's a word that's often misunderstood, especially when it comes to loss. For a long time, I thought that accepting my grief meant letting go of the person I loved. I thought it meant saying goodbye to the dreams I had for my future or turning away from the parts of myself that were broken by loss. But the truth is, acceptance is not about "getting over" your loss or forgetting what was once so important to you. Acceptance is about learning to live alongside your grief, to carry it with you in a way that allows you to keep moving forward.

When I lost Vince, I couldn't imagine ever accepting a world without him. The idea of "moving on" felt like a betrayal. How could I accept a life that no longer included him? But slowly, through countless painful moments and small steps, I began to understand that acceptance didn't mean erasing the past or even letting go of the grief I felt. It meant finding a way to live with it, to honor it, while still allowing myself to grow, to live, and to experience life in a new way.

What Acceptance Really Means

For many people, the word "acceptance" feels like an endpoint—a final destination where the pain fades and life returns to normal. But that's not how it works. Acceptance is not about reaching a point where you no longer feel the weight of your loss. It's not about closing the door on your grief and stepping into a future without it. Instead, acceptance is about finding peace with the fact that the loss will always be a part of your story, but it doesn't have to define every moment of your life.

I came to realize that acceptance isn't a single moment of epiphany where everything makes sense and the hurt disappears. It's a journey—one that's full of ups and downs, moments of clarity followed by waves of deep sadness. But over time, I learned that I could carry my grief without it consuming me. I could miss Vince, mourn the future we didn't get to have, and still allow myself to find new moments of joy and connection. Acceptance meant understanding that my life would never be the same, but that it could still be beautiful in a new way.

Carrying Your Grief with You

One of the most important lessons I've learned is that grief doesn't disappear. It changes, it evolves, but it doesn't just vanish once you reach a point of acceptance. And that's okay. We carry our grief with us, and it becomes part of who we are. But carrying your grief doesn't mean you're stuck in it. It doesn't mean you're doomed to a life of sadness. Instead, it means that you can hold your grief in one hand while reaching out for new experiences, new relationships, and new moments of joy with the other.

Grief is a part of your journey, but it doesn't define your entire story. Acceptance allows you to carry that grief with you while still finding space for growth, for love, for joy, and for hope.

The Coexistence of Love and Grief

One of the hardest parts of acceptance is understanding that love and grief can coexist. After a loss, it's easy to feel like you're stuck between two opposing forces—the love you still feel and the pain of that loss. But the truth is, they're not opposites. They are deeply intertwined. You grieve because you love. And that love doesn't disappear just because the person, the relationship, or the dream is no longer physically present in your life.

In fact, it's that very love that helps you heal. For a long time, I thought that accepting Vince's death meant somehow diminishing the love I had for him. But I came to realize that my love for him was still very much alive. It had simply transformed. It became part of the strength that helped me move forward. Acceptance allowed me to keep loving him while also making room in my heart for new experiences, new connections, new love and new possibilities.

This is true for any kind of loss. When a relationship ends, the love you felt doesn't just vanish. It becomes part of your story. It shapes you. And even though that relationship may no longer be part of your future, the love you experienced will always be part of your past. Acceptance allows you to hold onto that love without being held back by it.

Finding Meaning in the Journey of Acceptance

The journey of acceptance isn't about getting over your loss—it's about growing through it. It's about recognizing that you are forever changed by what you've lost, but that you still have the power to shape your future. It's about finding meaning in your grief, not by minimizing it, but by allowing it to guide you toward a deeper understanding of yourself and the world around you.

Acceptance doesn't mean that the pain goes away. There will still be days when the sadness feels overwhelming, when the weight of your loss feels heavier than ever. But acceptance means knowing that those moments are part of the process, and they don't define the entirety of your life. You are still here. You are still growing. And you are still capable of finding joy, connection, and meaning—even with your grief by your side.

Acceptance is not about "getting over" your loss. It's about learning to carry it with you as you continue to grow, live, and find new meaning. Your grief, your love, and your strength can coexist. You are allowed to feel both the weight of your sadness and the light of your future. Acceptance is not the end of your journey—it's the beginning of a new chapter, one where you are free to honor both what you've lost and what you still have to gain.

As you continue on this journey of grief, remember that acceptance is not a destination you must reach. It's a process, a journey, and it looks different for everyone. But through it all, know this: you are *brokenly beautiful*, and in the midst of your grief, you are also growing, healing, and finding new ways to live and love. You don't have to leave your grief behind—you can carry it with you as you step into the fullness of your life, with all its complexity, beauty, and possibility.

Chapter 15: Rediscovering Joy

After any profound loss—joy can feel like a distant memory. It's as if the light has been drained from the world, leaving only shadows and sorrow. I remember feeling as though the part of me that knew how to laugh, smile, and enjoy life had been lost too. How could I find joy again when so much had been taken from me?

For the longest time, I felt like I didn't deserve to be happy. The weight of my grief was so heavy that even the smallest moments of joy felt like a betrayal. I told myself that if I allowed myself to feel happiness, it would mean I was forgetting my loss. But that belief kept me trapped, living in a world of sorrow where joy felt like something reserved for other people—people who weren't hurting the way I was.

But here's what I discovered: joy and grief can coexist. In fact, they "must" coexist. Grief doesn't cancel out joy, and joy doesn't erase grief. They are both part of the human experience, and after a loss—no matter what kind of loss it is—allowing yourself to rediscover joy is one of the most powerful ways to heal.

The Guilt of Joy

When you've lost something or someone important, joy can feel like guilt. I remember the first time I laughed after Vince passed. It was over something small—a silly joke my son made at the dinner table—and before I knew it, I was laughing out loud. But the joy was short-lived, quickly replaced by a wave of guilt that hit me like a punch to the gut. How could I laugh when my world had been turned upside down? How could I find happiness when I was still drowning in grief?

This feeling isn't unique to grief from death. I've felt it after relationships ended, after dreams fell apart, and after plans unraveled. Each time, the guilt was there, whispering that I didn't have the right to be happy when things had gone so wrong. But here's the truth: *it's okay to feel joy again*. You are allowed to laugh, to smile, and to enjoy the small pleasures that life brings. Joy doesn't mean you've forgotten your loss—it means you are choosing to live alongside it.

Grief and joy can share the same space in your heart. They don't cancel each other out. You can still honor what you've lost and allow yourself to find beauty in the world again. You don't need to carry the weight of guilt along with your grief. By letting go of that guilt, you open yourself up to the possibility of healing.

The Power of Small Moments

When I first began to rediscover joy, it didn't come in big, life-changing moments. It came in whispers, in fleeting glimmers of light that felt almost fragile at first. It was the warmth of the sun on my face during a walk in the park. It was the smell of my morning coffee, the comfort of a favorite song, or the sound of the kids laughing. These moments were small, almost insignificant, but they were real. They reminded me that even in the midst of my pain, there was still beauty in the world.

Joy doesn't have to come in grand gestures. It can be found in the quiet moments—the ones that might have gone unnoticed before. Maybe it's the way the light filters through your window in the morning or the taste of your favorite food. Maybe it's the sound of a friend's voice on the phone or the feel of soft blankets at the end of a long day. These small moments of joy are the building blocks of healing.

Rediscovering joy after loss isn't about moving on or forgetting what you've lost. It's about embracing life in all its complexity—the highs and the lows, the joy and the pain. You are allowed to laugh again, to feel happiness, and to find beauty in the world, even after your heart has been broken. You are *brokenly beautiful*, and within that brokenness, there is still room for light. There is still room for joy.

Remember, joy doesn't erase your grief. It lives alongside it, and together they make you whole. Embrace those small moments of happiness without guilt. You deserve joy, even in the midst of your sorrow. And slowly, those moments will grow, and you'll find that joy is not something lost forever—it's something waiting to be rediscovered, one beautiful moment at a time.

Chapter 16: Creating a New Normal

After any profound loss—it can feel like your world has been completely shattered. The life you knew, the future you had envisioned, and the plans you had built now seem unreachable, lost in the haze of grief and uncertainty. I know that feeling all too well. After my own losses, I found myself standing in the rubble of what once was, asking the question that so many of us ask in those moments: "What now?"

Grief, in all its forms, leaves you feeling like nothing will ever be the same—and in many ways, it won't. But as I discovered, life after loss doesn't have to be defined by the absence of what was. It can be filled with new beginnings, new joys, and new purpose. The phrase "a new normal" often feels inadequate because there's nothing normal about rebuilding your life after loss. It's hard. It's messy. It's full of starts and stops. But it's also possible. And with time, you will create a life that is different—*yes*—but also beautiful.

The Struggle of Letting Go of the Old Life

In the wake of loss, one of the hardest things to do is let go of the life you thought you would have. I spent so much time holding onto the idea of what my life was "supposed" to look like. After Vince passed, I found myself thinking about all the plans we had made, the future we were supposed to share. After losing a relationship, I clung to the idea of what it could have been if things had gone differently. And after other personal losses, I grieved for the version of myself that I thought I would be.

It's natural to want to hold onto the past, to cling to what was familiar and comfortable. But in doing so, we prevent ourselves from fully stepping into what's possible. Letting go of the old life doesn't mean forgetting what you've lost—it means making space for something new.

It means allowing yourself to imagine a future that looks different, but still holds beauty and meaning.

Building a New Routine

One of the first steps in creating a new normal is building new routines. After a loss, the routines that once anchored your life may feel empty or unbearable. For me, mornings were the hardest. I had once woken up next to Vince every day, and without him, the mornings felt impossibly long and lonely. But over time, I began to create new routines—small rituals that brought me a sense of comfort and stability.

Maybe you used to have dinner with someone who is no longer there, or maybe your mornings were spent getting ready for a job you no longer have. Whatever your loss, it's important to create new routines that reflect the life you're living now. This might mean something as simple as starting a new hobby, taking a walk every day, or finding a new way to structure your time. These routines won't erase the pain of your loss, but they can help create a sense of order in the midst of chaos.

Finding Meaning in the New Chapter

One of the most challenging aspects of loss is the feeling that your life no longer has the same meaning it once did. The plans you had, the goals you were working toward, the future you were building—all of that can feel like it's been taken away. But here's the truth: you are allowed to find new meaning. You are allowed to dream new dreams. You are allowed to build a life that honors both the past and the future.

After my own losses, I found meaning in new ways. I discovered that while the path I had been on had changed, it didn't mean that my life was any less valuable or purposeful. I found purpose in my writing, in connecting with others who were also navigating grief, in sharing my story so that others would feel less alone. I found new ways to give love, to experience joy, and to contribute to the world around me.

Your loss, whatever it may be, does not define the rest of your life. It's part of your story, yes, but it's not the whole story. There is more ahead—more opportunities to grow, to connect, to find joy. And while the life you had planned may no longer be possible, a new life is waiting for you, one that can still be filled with beauty, love, and purpose.

Embracing Hope and the Future

One of the most important things I've learned on this journey is that it's okay to hope again. After loss, hope can feel fragile, like it might slip through your fingers if you reach for it. But it's there, waiting for you to embrace it. Hope doesn't mean you're forgetting what you've lost. It means you're allowing yourself to believe in the possibility of joy, love, and fulfillment once more.

It took time for me to allow myself to hope again. After my loss, I was afraid to dream, afraid to plan for the future because I wasn't sure if I could handle more disappointment. But slowly, as I built my new normal, I began to see that hope was not something to fear—it was something to nurture. It was a sign that I was healing, that I was ready to embrace life again, even with all its uncertainties.

It's okay to build a new life, one that honors both the past and the future. You are allowed to dream again, to hope again, to create a life that feels full even after loss. Your journey is not over. In fact, it's just beginning. The beauty of creating a new normal is that it's yours to define. It may look different from what you expected, but it can still be beautiful. You are *brokenly beautiful*, and in that brokenness, you will find strength, resilience, and the courage to move forward.

As you continue to navigate your own journey of loss, remember that you have the power to create a new normal. It won't happen all at once, and it won't always be easy, but step by step, you can build a life that honors both what you've lost and what you still have. You are allowed to change, to grow, to find meaning in this new chapter. And in time, you will discover that while life may be different, it can still be full of love, joy, and purpose. You are not just surviving—you are creating something beautiful.

Chapter 17: Healing is Not Linear

Healing is a journey, not a straight path to a final destination. It's more like a winding road, full of twists, turns, setbacks, and unexpected moments of clarity. Some days you'll feel like you're making real progress, like you're finally finding your footing again. Other days, it'll feel like the ground has been ripped out from under you, and the grief will crash over you like a wave, knocking the wind out of you when you least expect it.

I wish I could tell you that healing happens in a smooth, predictable way—that there's a point where the pain just stops, and you can move forward without looking back. But that's not how it works. Healing is messy. It's filled with moments of hope and moments of despair, and sometimes it feels like you're taking two steps forward and three steps back. But even when it feels like you're moving backward, trust that you "are" healing. Even in the setbacks, even in the hardest moments, you are still on your path to healing.

The Illusion of Progress

After Vince passed, I thought healing would be a steady climb—slow but consistent. I believed that with enough time, the pain would gradually lessen until it was gone. But that's not what happened. There were days when I felt strong, when I believed I was making progress, and then, without warning, the grief would hit me all over again, just as sharp and overwhelming as the day I lost him. It felt like I was starting from scratch, like all the progress I had made was erased in an instant.

But here's what I've learned: those setbacks, those moments when the grief comes rushing back, are "part" of the healing process. Healing doesn't happen in a straight line. It's full of ups and downs, and that's normal. Some days you'll feel okay. Some days you'll laugh, you'll smile, you'll even feel like yourself again. And other days, you'll feel the weight of your loss all over again. Both of these experiences are valid, and both are part of the journey.

The Importance of Self-Compassion

When you're healing, one of the most important things you can do is to show yourself compassion. It's easy to get frustrated with yourself when you feel like you're not "making progress" or when the pain comes back unexpectedly. But healing isn't about being perfect, and it's not about reaching a point where the pain is completely gone. It's about learning to live with the pain in a way that doesn't consume you. It's about giving yourself grace on the days when you feel like you're moving backward.

Self-compassion means being kind to yourself when things are hard. It means recognizing that healing is a difficult, ongoing process, and it's okay to have setbacks. You don't have to be "better" all the time. You don't have to have it all together. You are allowed to feel sad, to have hard days, and to give yourself the space to heal at your own pace.

Practice Self-Compassion

The next time you feel like you're not making progress in your healing, take a moment to pause and remind yourself that healing isn't a race. You are not falling behind. You are exactly where you need to be on your journey. Write down three things you appreciate about yourself, or three things you've done that have shown strength, even if they seem small. Remind yourself that healing takes time and that you are allowed to go at your own pace.

The Power of Resilience

Resilience doesn't mean that you never feel pain. It doesn't mean that you are immune to setbacks or that you always move forward without faltering. Resilience is about getting back up, even after you've been knocked down. It's about trusting that you have the strength to carry on, even when the journey feels overwhelming. And it's about knowing that every time you get back up, you are healing.

After a loss, you may feel like you'll never be the same—and in many ways, you won't be. But that doesn't mean you're not resilient. In fact, your ability to continue moving forward, even in the face of such immense pain, is a testament to your resilience. You don't have to be "strong" in the traditional sense. You just have to keep going, one step at a time.

Healing is not a linear process, and that's okay. You are allowed to have setbacks, to feel sad, to stumble along the way. But through it all, remember that you are healing. You are growing. You are learning to live with your grief in a way that honors both your pain and your strength. You are *brokenly beautiful*, and within that brokenness, there is resilience, there is growth, and there is hope. Keep going, even on the hard days. You are stronger than you know, and you are healing, even when it doesn't feel like it.

Chapter 18: Moving Forward with Grace

As you reach this chapter, you've walked through some of the most challenging experiences of your life. You've navigated the weight of grief, the complexity of emotions, and the process of finding yourself again after loss. But what comes next? How do you move forward with grace, carrying both the pain of what you've lost and the hope of what lies ahead?

Moving forward doesn't mean leaving your grief behind. It doesn't mean you're closing a chapter and forgetting what you've been through. Instead, it means embracing the idea that life continues, and so do you. You are different now—reshaped by loss, by love, by the lessons you've learned along the way. Moving forward with grace is about carrying all of that with you, with an open heart and a sense of compassion for yourself and your journey.

The Power of Self-Compassion

One of the most important elements of moving forward is self-compassion. After loss, it's easy to be hard on yourself—to feel like you should be further along in your healing or to criticize yourself for still feeling pain. But grace begins with kindness. It begins with allowing yourself to be exactly where you are, without judgment. Healing is not a race, and there is no finish line. Moving forward with grace means letting go of the need for perfection and accepting the ebb and flow of your emotions.

In moments of self-doubt, remember all that you've been through and all the strength it has taken to get you here. Each step you've taken—no matter how small—is a testament to your resilience. And as you continue to move forward, allow that same compassion to guide you. Be gentle with yourself, especially on the hard days. Grace is not about having it all together—it's about honoring where you are, while still holding space for where you're going.

Honoring What You've Lost While Embracing What's Ahead

Moving forward doesn't mean forgetting what you've lost. The people, dreams, and parts of yourself that you've had to say goodbye to will always be a part of your story. But there's room in your life for both the love of what's gone and the hope of what's to come. It's not about choosing one or the other—it's about making space for both.

I've learned that it's possible to honor Vince's memory while still allowing myself to create new memories. It's possible to cherish the dreams I had while opening my heart to new possibilities. Moving forward with grace means finding that balance—honoring the past while also embracing the present and future.

There will be moments when the grief resurfaces, when the weight of loss feels heavy again. And that's okay. Grace allows for those moments. It makes room for both the joy and the sorrow. It's not about moving on—it's about moving forward, with all the pieces of your heart.

Trusting the Process of Growth

One of the hardest parts of moving forward is trusting that you are growing, even when it doesn't feel like it. Healing doesn't happen in a straight line. There will be setbacks, moments when you feel like you've taken a step backward. But growth is still happening, even in those moments.

Trust that every experience—every high and every low—is part of your journey. Trust that the pain you've felt has not been in vain, that it is shaping you into someone who is more compassionate, more understanding, and more deeply connected to the world around you.

Moving forward with grace means surrendering to the process, knowing that growth is happening even when it's hard to see.

Carrying Hope as You Move Forward

Perhaps the most important part of moving forward with grace is carrying hope with you. After loss, hope can feel fragile, like something that might slip through your fingers if you reach for it. But hope is resilient, just like you. It's the quiet belief that there is still beauty to be found, still joy to be experienced, still love to be shared.

As you move forward, allow hope to be your companion. Even on the days when it feels distant, know that it is still there, waiting for you. Hope doesn't mean that everything will be perfect—it simply means that there is still possibility, still light to be found even after the darkest moments.

Encouragement for the Road Ahead

As you continue on your journey, remember this: You are not defined by your loss. You are defined by how you choose to move forward, by the grace you carry within you, and by the love that remains in your heart. You are *brokenly beautiful*, and in that brokenness, you have found strength, resilience, and hope.

Moving forward doesn't mean you're leaving anything behind—it means you're carrying it with you, woven into the fabric of who you are. So move forward with grace, with compassion, and with an open heart. There is still so much life to be lived, still so much love to be felt, and still so much beauty to be discovered.

You are stronger than you know. And with each step you take, you are creating a life that honors both the love you've lost and the possibilities that still lie ahead.

Chapter 19: Living with Love and Loss

Grief is not something that simply disappears with time. It doesn't have an expiration date, and it doesn't fade away like a distant memory. It becomes part of who you are. The truth is that grief never fully leaves you. But here's the beauty in that truth: grief, when held with tenderness and love, can coexist with joy, hope, and the promise of the future.

I used to believe that I had to choose. That either I could honor my grief and live in the past, or I could move forward and embrace the present and future without looking back. But I learned something so powerful along the way: *you don't have to choose*. You can live with both love and loss. You can honor what you've lost while also allowing yourself to love, to laugh, and to find joy again.

For me, Vince's memory will always be a part of me, like a thread woven into the fabric of my soul. But over time, I realized that grief didn't have to be my only companion. I could carry his memory with me "and" still open myself to new experiences, new relationships, and new moments of joy. And this truth isn't just for those of us who have lost someone to death. It's for anyone who has experienced profound loss—the end of a relationship you once cherished, the shattering of a dream you held dear, or the loss of a part of yourself that defined you.

Living with both love and loss is not just possible—it's beautiful. And it's what makes you "brokenly beautiful".

Grief Doesn't End, It Changes

One of the most comforting things I've learned is that grief doesn't end, but it does change. In the beginning, it can feel like a constant ache, a weight that never leaves your chest. But over time, grief begins to shift. It becomes something softer, something you can carry alongside everything else. It's still there, but it no longer consumes you the way it once did.

I'll always carry Vince's memory with me—his laugh, his warmth, the way he made me feel safe. But I no longer carry the same sharp pain that I once did. The grief has settled, like waves that have finally calmed after a storm. And in that calm, I've found space for other things. I've found space for new memories, for new love, for new joys that have their own place in my heart. The grief didn't disappear—it simply made room for everything else.

This is your journey too. Your grief will change. You will carry it with you, but it will soften. And in that softening, you will find room to live fully again. You will find space to love again, even while honoring what you've lost.

When we experience profound loss, it's easy to feel like we have to let go of one to make room for the other. But love and loss are intertwined. You grieve because you love, and that love doesn't just vanish. It changes form, but it doesn't disappear. The memories you hold, the lessons you've learned, and the love that remains all shape how you move forward.

I realized that I didn't have to let go of my grief to experience joy again. I could honor my love for Vince while also opening my heart to new possibilities. This realization was freeing. It allowed me to stop fighting the grief and instead make space for both love and loss to coexist. And in that coexistence, I found a new way of living—one that honors what I've lost while also embracing what I still have.

You don't have to choose between love and loss. You can carry both. You can honor what you've lost while still finding joy, love, and connection in the world around you. Your grief doesn't have to define your life—it can become part of a larger, more complex story. You are "brokenly beautiful", and within that brokenness, there is still room for joy, love, and hope.

As you continue on your journey, remember that grief doesn't end, but it does change. You can live with it, alongside everything else that makes life worth living. You are allowed to grieve, and you are allowed to laugh. You are allowed to carry both your sorrow and your joy. And in doing so, you honor the full complexity of what it means to live and love.

Chapter 20: Grieving While Parenting – A Child's Journey Through Loss

Grief is complex enough for adults to navigate, but when it comes to children, it can feel even more overwhelming. As parents, we want to protect our children from pain, to shield them from the harsh realities of life. But loss doesn't discriminate by age. Children grieve, too. They may not have the words to fully express their feelings, and they might not understand the permanence of death or the intricacies of loss, but the pain is still there, quietly shaping their world.

My son was only six when we lost his father. He was just beginning to understand the world, and suddenly, the foundation of his reality shifted in ways no child should have to face. In those early days, I worried constantly about how this loss would affect him. Would he remember his father? Would he be able to process what had happened? How could I possibly guide him through something that I was struggling to navigate myself?

Children grieve differently. Sometimes their sadness comes out in short bursts—a moment of quiet confusion, a sudden question, a change in behavior. Other times, they seem completely unaffected, playing as if nothing has changed. But the truth is, they are processing the loss in their own way, on their own timeline, and it's our job as parents to create a space where they feel safe to express whatever they're feeling.

Helping Your Child Grieve

One of the hardest things I've had to do as a parent is help my son grieve while dealing with my own overwhelming sadness. How do you answer questions you barely know the answers to yourself? How do you find the strength to support your child when your own heart feels shattered? I remember Vinnie asking "Where did daddy go?", "Is he getting a ticket back to earth""

The truth is, you don't have to have all the answers. You don't have to be perfectly composed or know the right things to say. What matters most is that your child knows it's okay to feel whatever they're feeling—that it's okay to be sad, to be confused, to be angry, or even to be happy. Children need to see that grief is not something to be feared or hidden away. It's something to be felt, to be talked about, and to be shared.

After the loss of Vince, I worried constantly that my son would forget him, that as the years passed, the memories would fade until his father became nothing more than a distant idea. But children remember in their own way. They remember through stories, through photos, through the little details that seem insignificant but hold the essence of a loved one.

We began creating new rituals—small ways to keep his father's memory alive. Lighting a candle on his birthday, sharing stories at dinner, looking at pictures together—these moments helped my son hold onto his father's presence in a way that felt comforting, not overwhelming. It became a way for him to grieve openly, to ask questions, and to understand that while his father was no longer physically with us, the love between them would never go away.

I used to worry that this early experience of loss would leave a permanent scar on my son—that it would shape him in ways I couldn't protect him from. And maybe it has. But over time, I've come to realize that grief, while painful, can also be a source of strength. My son is compassionate beyond his years. He understands the fragility of life in a way that many adults don't. His experience of loss has made him empathetic, kind, and deeply aware of the love we share while we have it.

Children may grieve differently, but they are resilient. And while we can't shield them from loss, we can teach them that grief is a part of life—a part that, though painful, is also an expression of the love we hold for those who are no longer with us.

In many ways, my son has taught me more about grief than I could have ever taught him. Children have a way of moving through the world with an openness and vulnerability that adults often struggle to embrace. They don't hide their feelings, they don't push their grief away, and they don't feel guilty for experiencing moments of joy even in the midst of loss. They grieve with their whole hearts, and in doing so, they show us how to hold both the sadness and the light.

I've learned that it's okay to let my son see me cry. It's okay to admit when I don't have all the answers. It's okay to let him be a part of my grief, just as I am a part of his. Together, we've learned that grief isn't something to be overcome—it's something to be carried, gently, with love, as we move forward.

Grieving while parenting is one of the hardest things I've ever had to do. It's a delicate balance between honoring your own sorrow while being present for your child's. But in the midst of the pain, there is also beauty. The beauty of shared memories, of love that transcends loss, and of watching your child grow stronger and more compassionate because of the very thing that once seemed too painful to bear.

Our children teach us that it's okay to grieve, to feel, and to find joy again. They remind us that life, even after loss, is still full of love, laughter, and connection. My son has taught me that grief, though heavy, can be carried with grace. And for that, I am eternally grateful.

Conclusion

Grief is not a destination. It's not something you "get over" or leave behind. It becomes a part of you—a constant companion that shifts and changes as you move through life. It's messy and painful, but within that pain, there is profound beauty. You may feel broken, shattered even, by the losses you've experienced—But here's what I want you to carry with you, every single day: "you are brokenly beautiful."

Your brokenness doesn't diminish you. It adds depth, strength, and resilience to who you are. It's in those cracks, in the places where life has hurt you most, that your true beauty shines through. You've faced heartbreak, you've endured unimaginable pain, and yet you're still standing. You are stronger than you know. The very fact that you've carried on, that you've continued to seek light even when the darkness felt overwhelming—that is the essence of what makes you so incredibly beautiful.

Grief is a lifelong journey, but it's one that you don't have to walk alone. There is no weakness in asking for help, in leaning on those who love you, or in seeking the support of a therapist or a community who understands what you're going through. You deserve to be held, to be supported, and to know that you are never truly alone in your pain. Your vulnerability, your willingness to keep going despite everything—this is where your strength lies.

As you move forward, know that it's okay to feel both grief and joy. It's okay to carry your loss with you while also making room for new experiences, new love, and new joy. You are not betraying your grief by finding happiness again. In fact, living fully, loving deeply, and embracing the beauty that still exists in this world is one of the most powerful ways to honor what you've lost. Your grief doesn't have to define you—it can transform you.

There will be days when the pain feels overwhelming, when the weight of your loss feels too heavy to bear. On those days, remember this: you are not broken beyond repair. You are "brokenly beautiful", and it's in those cracks that the light gets in. It's in those cracks that healing begins. You are allowed to laugh, to love, to cry, and to feel every emotion that comes your way. You are allowed to live a life that honors both the love and the loss, the joy and the sorrow.

So as you continue this journey, carry this with you every day: "You are stronger than you know. There is beauty in your brokenness. And even in the midst of grief, you are allowed to live fully, to love deeply, and to embrace the beauty that still exists in this world."

You are not defined by your losses, but by how you rise from them. Your story, your heart, and your soul are a testament to the fact that brokenness is not the end—it's where you begin to rebuild. And in that rebuilding, in that healing, you are more beautiful than ever before.

You are "brokenly beautiful", and that, is your strength.